C. SERAPHIM

St. Michael the Archangel Prayer Book

Nine Days With St. Michael the Archangel

First edition

This book was professionally typeset on Reedsy.
Find out more at reedsy.com

Contents

1

Story of St. Michael

MI-CA-EL, or "Who is like unto God?" was the cry of the great Archangel when he smote the rebel Lucifer in the battle of the angelic hosts. From that hour he has been known as Michael, Captain of the armies of God, the embodiment of divine fortitude, the champion of every devout soul in strife with the forces of evil.

According to the ancient tale, a heavenly battle unfolded after the creation of the heavens and earth. Lucifer, also known as the "light-bearer" and the "morning star," held a prominent position among the angels but harbored envy and pride. He rebelled against God, driven by his desire to seize God's throne and reject His authority. In his insurrection, Lucifer convinced a third of the angels to join his cause. However, Michael remained steadfastly loyal to God, declaring his undying service, for "who is like unto God" ("Michael"). With the support of the remaining two-thirds of the angels, Michael successfully thwarted Lucifer's rebellion, casting him and his followers out of heaven. From that moment onward, Lucifer became known as Satan, and his angelic supporters transformed into devils. In recognition of Michael's unwavering loyalty, God elevated him to the position of chief angel. The Church, acknowledging his leadership, later bestowed upon him the title of a Saint, while the Eastern Liturgy referred to him as the "Archistrategos" or the "highest general."

2

Offices of St. Michael

Saint Michael, the Archangel, holds a prominent position among angels, recognized widely for his role and significance. In addition to Saint Gabriel and Saint Raphael, he belongs to the esteemed rank of Archangels, denoting his status as a chief angel. Saint Michael's reverence extends beyond Christian tradition, encompassing Jewish and Islamic faiths as well.

The name "Michael" carries the profound meaning of "who is like unto God." Meanwhile, the Greek term "Angelos" translates to "messenger." Angels, as ethereal beings, engage in the dual purpose of praising God and serving as intermediaries between the divine and humanity. Furthermore, they shoulder the responsibility of safeguarding nations, communities, and individuals. Throughout Sacred Scripture, angels are referenced on 192 occasions, and classified into nine distinct categories. Within this extensive mention, Saint Michael's name is specifically recorded four times;

1) Daniel 10:13 ~ But the prince (that is the guardian angel of Persia) of the kingdom of the Persians resisted me one and twenty days, and behold Michael, one of the chief princes, came to help me...

2) Daniel 12:1 ~ But at that time (end of the world) shall Michael rise up, the great prince, who stands up for the children of your people.

3) Jude 1:9 ~ Yet when Michael the archangel was fiercely disputing with the devil about the body of Moses...

4) Apocalypse (Revelation) 12:7 - 9 ~ And there was a battle in heaven: Michael and his angels battled with the dragon, and although the dragon and his angels. fought back, they were overpowered and lost their place in heaven. The huge dragon, the ancient serpent known as the devil or Satan, the seducer of the whole world, was driven out and hurled down to earth and his minions with him.

From these passages, four offices are often assigned to St. Michael:

- To fight against Satan and evil.

- To rescue the souls of the faithful from the power of the devil.

- To be the champion of God's people.

- To summon people's souls from this earth and bring them to judgment.

Apart from his prominent military role, St. Michael also acquired the attribution of a healer. This tradition originated in Phrygia, where numerous healing hot springs were dedicated to him. Over time, Constantinople revered him as a celestial doctor. As the centuries passed, St. Michael was invoked in various other capacities.

In Egypt, he became the patron of the Nile, and his feast day was celebrated when the river began to rise. Germany and France held him in special veneration, particularly in rugged natural landscapes, such as mountains, with Mont St. Michael in Brittany being the most renowned site. Portugal recognizes him as its guardian, observing his feast day on the third Sunday of June with special permission from the Pope. Among his many titles are Prince, Angel of Chivalry, Angel of Judgment, and Angel of the Sun.

3

Veneration of St. Michael

The veneration of St. Michael has deep roots, extending back to ancient times. Even among the Jewish people, he held a revered status as the patron of Israel, and his presence featured prominently in Hebraic Kabbal and other mystical writings and traditions.

In Christianity, the cult of St. Michael gained significant recognition during the fourth century. Pope Sylvester in Rome and Patriarch Alexander in Alexandria both introduced the feast dedicated to him. In the Western Church, the Feast of Saint Michael, along with Saint Gabriel, Saint Raphael, and all the Archangels, is celebrated on September 29th, while the Eastern Church observes the same feast on November 8th.

During the reign of Constantine the Great (324 - 337), the first Roman emperor to embrace Christianity, a church was constructed in honor of St. Michael on the Bosphorus at a location known as Anaplus, situated around fifty miles south of Constantinople. On the opposite headland, on the Asiatic shore, Emperor Justinian built yet another church dedicated to St. Michael. In Constantinople and its surrounding areas alone, numerous churches and chapels, approximately fifteen in number, were erected in honor of this Archangel during the fourth and fifth centuries. Other cities and towns soon followed suit. For instance, Ravenna constructed a large church in honor of St. Michael and celebrated his feast on June 9th. During the reign of Emperor Arcadius, another renowned church was built in Constantinople near healing springs. It was dedicated to St. Michael and the entire assembly of angels, known as the "synaxis" or synod. This particular feast, the Synaxis of St. Michael and all the angels was celebrated on November 8th and emerged as the primary date for venerating the Archangel in the Eastern Church. The observance of this feast quickly spread throughout the Greek, Syrian, and Coptic Churches.

Both Western paintings and Eastern iconography depict St. Michael in certain consistent artistic ways. He is typically depicted with a halo, symbolizing his sanctity, and wings, as is customary for most angels.

The concept of angels being portrayed with wings originated relatively late in Judaism, emerging after the Babylonian captivity. The winged lions and bulls of the Assyrians, as well as the griffins of the Hittites, had an influence on the Israelites, contributing to the adoption of winged imagery for angels. In Western art, St. Michael is often depicted carrying a sword, representing his victory over Satan and evil. Additionally, he may be shown holding a scale, symbolizing his role in the final judgment. Frequently, a horned, winged Satan or dragon is depicted beneath his feet, being trampled and defeated. These portrayals often include a depiction of a fiery abyss, symbolizing hell as the intended destiny of the devil.

In Eastern icons, although some do feature St. Michael holding a scale or sword, triumphing over evil, he is predominantly depicted holding a staff and/or an orb. These symbols represent his roles as a messenger, seer, and his wise and insightful governance. His countenance is fair and noble, and his overall pose exudes a sense of peace and ethereal beauty.

4

Prayers to St. Michael

St. Michael Novena Day 1

Let us begin, In the name of the Father, and of the Son, and of the Holy Spirit. Amen.

O glorious prince Saint Michael, chief and commander of the heavenly hosts, guardian of souls, vanquisher of rebel spirits, servant in the house of the Divine King, and our admirable conductor, you who shine with excellence and superhuman virtue, deliver us from all evil. We turn to you with confidence and seek your gracious protection to help us serve God more faithfully each day. Pray for us, O glorious Saint Michael, Prince of the Church of Jesus Christ, that we may be worthy of His promises.

(Mention your request here...)

Almighty and Everlasting God, by your great goodness and desire for the salvation of all humanity, you have appointed the most glorious Archangel Saint Michael as the Prince of Your Church. We ask you to make us worthy to be delivered from all our enemies, so that none may harass us at the hour of death. May St. Michael guide us into Your presence. We ask this through the merits of Jesus Christ Our Lord.

Amen.

Saint Michael the Archangel, defend us in battle, be our protection against the wickedness and snares of the devil. We humbly pray that God rebuke him, and you, O Prince of the Heavenly host, by the power of God, cast Satan and all evil spirits into Hell, who roam about the world seeking the ruin of souls.

Amen.

Say 1: Our Father... Say 1: Hail Mary... Say 1: Glory Be...

St. Michael Novena Day 2

Let us begin, In the name of the Father, and of the Son, and of the Holy Spirit. Amen.

O glorious prince Saint Michael, chief and commander of the heavenly hosts, guardian of souls, vanquisher of rebel spirits, servant in the house of the Divine King, and our admirable conductor, you who shine with excellence and superhuman virtue, deliver us from all evil. We turn to you with confidence and seek your gracious protection to help us serve God more faithfully each day. Pray for us, O glorious Saint Michael, Prince of the Church of Jesus Christ, that we may be worthy of His promises.

(Mention your request here...)

Almighty and Everlasting God, by your great goodness and merciful desire for the salvation of all humanity, you have appointed the most glorious Archangel Saint Michael as the Prince of Your Church. We ask you to make us worthy to be delivered from all our enemies, so that none may harass us at the hour of death. May we be guided by St. Michael into Your presence. We ask this through the merits of Jesus Christ Our Lord.

Amen.

Saint Michael the Archangel, defend us in battle, be our protection against the wickedness and snares of the devil. We humbly pray that God rebuke him, and you, O Prince of the Heavenly host, by the power of God, cast Satan and all evil spirits into Hell, who roam about the world seeking the ruin of souls.

Amen.

Say 1: Our Father... Say 1: Hail Mary... Say 1: Glory Be...

St. Michael Novena Day 3

Let us begin, In the name of the Father, and of the Son, and of the Holy Spirit. Amen.

O glorious prince Saint Michael, chief and commander of the heavenly hosts, guardian of souls, vanquisher of rebel spirits, servant in the house of the Divine King, and our admirable conductor, you who shine with excellence and superhuman virtue, deliver us from all evil. We turn to you with confidence and seek your gracious protection to help us serve God more faithfully each day. Pray for us, O glorious Saint Michael, Prince of the Church of Jesus Christ, that we may be worthy of His promises.

(Mention your request here...)

Almighty and Everlasting God, by your great goodness and merciful desire for the salvation of all humanity, you have appointed the most glorious Archangel Saint Michael as the Prince of Your Church. We ask you to make us worthy to be delivered from all our enemies, so that none may harass us at the hour of death. May we be conducted by St. Michael into Your presence. We ask this through the merits of Jesus Christ Our Lord.

Amen.

Saint Michael the Archangel, defend us in battle, be our protection against the wickedness and snares of the devil. We humbly pray that God rebuke him, and you, O Prince of the Heavenly host, by the power of God, cast Satan and all evil spirits into Hell, who roam about the world seeking the ruin of souls.

Amen.

Say 1: Our Father... Say 1: Hail Mary... Say 1: Glory Be...

St. Michael Novena Day 4

Let us begin, In the name of the Father, and of the Son, and of the Holy Spirit. Amen.

O glorious prince Saint Michael, chief and commander of the heavenly hosts, guardian of souls, vanquisher of rebel spirits, servant in the house of the Divine King, and our admirable conductor, you who shine with excellence and superhuman virtue, deliver us from all evil. We turn to you with confidence and seek your gracious protection to help us serve God more faithfully each day. Pray for us, O glorious Saint Michael, Prince of the Church of Jesus Christ, that we may be worthy of His promises.

(Mention your request here...)

Almighty and Everlasting God, by your great goodness and merciful desire for the salvation of all humanity, you have appointed the most glorious Archangel Saint Michael as the Prince of Your Church. We ask you to make us worthy to be delivered from all our enemies, so that none may harass us at the hour of death. May we be conducted by St. Michael into Your presence. We ask this through the merits of Jesus Christ Our Lord.

Amen.

Saint Michael the Archangel, defend us in battle, be our protection against the wickedness and snares of the devil. We humbly pray that God rebuke him, and you, O Prince of the Heavenly host, by the power of God, cast Satan and all evil spirits into Hell, who roam about the world seeking the ruin of souls.

Amen.

Say 1: Our Father... Say 1: Hail Mary... Say 1: Glory Be...

St. Michael Novena Day 5

Let us begin, In the name of the Father, and of the Son, and of the Holy Spirit. Amen.

O glorious prince Saint Michael, chief and commander of the heavenly hosts, guardian of souls, vanquisher of rebel spirits, servant in the house of the Divine King, and our admirable conductor, you who shine with excellence and superhuman virtue, deliver us from all evil. We turn to you with confidence and seek your gracious protection to help us serve God more faithfully each day. Pray for us, O glorious Saint Michael, Prince of the Church of Jesus Christ, that we may be worthy of His promises.

(Mention your request here...)

Almighty and Everlasting God, by your great goodness and merciful desire for the salvation of all humanity, you have appointed the most glorious Archangel Saint Michael as the Prince of Your Church. We ask you to make us worthy to be delivered from all our enemies, so that none may harass us at the hour of death. May we be conducted by St. Michael into Your presence. We ask this through the merits of Jesus Christ Our Lord.

Amen.

Saint Michael the Archangel, defend us in battle, be our protection against the wickedness and snares of the devil. We humbly pray that God rebuke him, and you, O Prince of the Heavenly host, by the power of God, cast Satan and all evil spirits into Hell, who roam about the world seeking the ruin of souls.

Amen.

Say 1: Our Father... Say 1: Hail Mary... Say 1: Glory Be...

St. Michael Novena Day 6

Let us begin, In the name of the Father, and of the Son, and of the Holy Spirit. Amen.

O glorious prince Saint Michael, chief and commander of the heavenly hosts, guardian of souls, vanquisher of rebel spirits, servant in the house of the Divine King, and our admirable conductor, you who shine with excellence and superhuman virtue, deliver us from all evil. We turn to you with confidence and seek your gracious protection to help us serve God more faithfully each day. Pray for us, O glorious Saint Michael, Prince of the Church of Jesus Christ, that we may be worthy of His promises.

(Mention your request here...)

Almighty and Everlasting God, by your great goodness and merciful desire for the salvation of all humanity, you have appointed the most glorious Archangel Saint Michael as the Prince of Your Church. We ask you to make us worthy to be delivered from all our enemies, so that none may harass us at the hour of death. May we be conducted by St. Michael into Your presence. We ask this through the merits of Jesus Christ Our Lord.

Amen.

Saint Michael the Archangel, defend us in battle, be our protection against the wickedness and snares of the devil. We humbly pray that God rebuke him, and you, O Prince of the Heavenly host, by the power of God, cast Satan and all evil spirits into Hell, who roam about the world seeking the ruin of souls.

Amen.

Say 1: Our Father... Say 1: Hail Mary... Say 1: Glory Be...

St. Michael Novena Day 7

Let us begin, In the name of the Father, and of the Son, and of the Holy Spirit. Amen.

O glorious prince Saint Michael, chief and commander of the heavenly hosts, guardian of souls, vanquisher of rebel spirits, servant in the house of the Divine King, and our admirable conductor, you who shine with excellence and superhuman virtue, deliver us from all evil. We turn to you with confidence and seek your gracious protection to help us serve God more faithfully each day. Pray for us, O glorious Saint Michael, Prince of the Church of Jesus Christ, that we may be made worthy of His promises.

(Mention your request here...)

Almighty and Everlasting God, by your great goodness and merciful desire for the salvation of all humanity, you have appointed the most glorious Archangel Saint Michael as the Prince of Your Church. We ask you to make us worthy to be delivered from all our enemies, that none of them may harass us at the hour of death. May we be conducted by him into Your presence. We ask this through the merits of Jesus Christ Our Lord.

Amen.

Saint Michael the Archangel, defend us in battle, be our protection against the wickedness and snares of the devil. May God rebuke him, and you, O Prince of the Heavenly host, by the power of God, cast Satan and all evil spirits into Hell, who prowl about the world seeking the ruin of souls.

Amen.

Say 1: Our Father... Say 1: Hail Mary... Say 1: Glory Be...

St. Michael Novena Day 8

Let us begin, In the name of the Father, and of the Son, and of the Holy Spirit. Amen.

O glorious prince Saint Michael, chief and commander of the heavenly hosts, guardian of souls, vanquisher of rebel spirits, servant in the house of the Divine King, and our admirable conductor, you who shine with excellence and superhuman virtue, deliver us from all evil. We turn to you with confidence and seek your gracious protection to help us serve God more faithfully each day. Pray for us, O glorious Saint Michael, Prince of the Church of Jesus Christ, that we may be made worthy of His promises.

(Mention your request here...)

Almighty and Everlasting God, by your great goodness and merciful desire for the salvation of all humanity, you have appointed the most glorious Archangel Saint Michael as the Prince of Your Church. We ask you to make us worthy to be delivered from all our enemies, that none of them may harass us at the hour of death. May we be conducted by him into Your presence. We ask this through the merits of Jesus Christ Our Lord.

Amen.

Saint Michael the Archangel, defend us in battle, be our protection against the wickedness and snares of the devil. May God rebuke him, and you, O Prince of the Heavenly host, by the power of God, cast Satan and all evil spirits into Hell, who prowl about the world seeking the ruin of souls.

Amen.

Say 1: Our Father... Say 1: Hail Mary... Say 1: Glory Be...

St. Michael Novena Day 9

Let us begin, In the name of the Father, and of the Son, and of the Holy Spirit. Amen.

O glorious prince Saint Michael, chief and commander of the heavenly hosts, guardian of souls, vanquisher of rebel spirits, servant in the house of the Divine King, and our admirable conductor, you who shine with excellence and superhuman virtue, deliver us from all evil. We turn to you with confidence and seek your gracious protection to help us serve God more faithfully each day. Pray for us, O glorious Saint Michael, Prince of the Church of Jesus Christ, that we may be made worthy of His promises.

(Mention your request here...)

Almighty and Everlasting God, by your great goodness and merciful desire for the salvation of all humanity, you have appointed the most glorious Archangel Saint Michael as the Prince of Your Church. We ask you to make us worthy to be delivered from all our enemies, that none of them may harass us at the hour of death. May we be conducted by him into Your presence. We ask this through the merits of Jesus Christ Our Lord.

Amen.

Saint Michael the Archangel, defend us in battle, be our protection against the wickedness and snares of the devil. May God rebuke him, and you, O Prince of the Heavenly host, by the power of God, cast Satan and all evil spirits into Hell, who prowl about the world seeking the ruin of souls.

Amen.

Say 1: Our Father... Say 1: Hail Mary... Say 1: Glory Be...

Printed in Great Britain
by Amazon

35803647R00015